OWASCO

PASSAGE
OF
LAKE
POEMS

PAUL B. ROTH

Finishing Line Press
Georgetown, Kentucky

OWASCO

PASSAGE
OF
LAKE
POEMS

Copyright © 2018 by Paul B. Roth
ISBN 978-1-63534-679-4 First Edition
All rights reserved under International and Pan-American Copyright Conventions. No part of this book may be reproduced in any manner whatsoever without written permission from the publisher, except in the case of brief quotations embodied in critical articles and reviews.

ACKNOWLEDGMENTS

Ann Arbor Review: "Backtracking," "Silence, Silence," "Without Ever Going Back," "Before Falling Asleep," "The One," "Futility," "Look No Further," "Thirst"
Many Mountains Moving: "Lake Spider"
Mudfish: "Apple Season in Central New York"
Osiris: "Speechless Among Stars," "Life Signs," "An Unheard of Silence," "Memoire"
Poet Lore: "Naming Silence"

Publisher: Leah Maines
Editor: Christen Kincaid
Cover Art: Paul B. Roth
Author Photo: Silvia Scheibli
Cover Design: Elizabeth Maines McCleavy

Printed in the USA on acid-free paper.
Order online: www.finishinglinepress.com
also available on amazon.com

Author inquiries and mail orders:
Finishing Line Press
P. O. Box 1626
Georgetown, Kentucky 40324
U. S. A.

Table of Contents

Backtracking 1
After the Storm 2
Positive Resignation 3
Speechless Among Stars 4
Life Signs 5
Edge 6
Some Belief 7
Attraction 8
Readiness 9
Rescue 10
A Night Vision 11
Water Stone 12
Naming Silence 13
Lake Spider 14
Silence, Silence 15
Water Depth 16
Without Ever Going Back 17
Apple Season in Central New York 18
Night Owl 19
Before Falling Asleep 20
Timed 21
Staying Put 22
An Unheard of Silence 23
The One 24
Moth Sonatina 25
Futility 26
Mémoire 27
Look No Further 28
Thirst 29
Death Yet 30

Backtracking

Owasco
how your waters
swarm
mirages of moonlight
through oak leaves
where I stand
tonight

How
this same light
breaking
my own body
into pieces

heals it
seamlessly
below
your overlapping
waves

How the Iroquois
named you
Owasco : Passage
long before
Christian missionaries
sipped

your ripples' edge
running cold
against their bleeding
blue lips

and with their rough
burlap sleeves
wiped their mouths
dry of you

After the Storm

Free
of itself
the moon
no longer
appears

Waves
perforate
its last light
below steep
rock cliffs
rising behind us

Ripples
the lips of fish
push up
to this lake's
surface

flatten out
into overlapping
rhythms
crickets mimic
at our backs
on shore

Positive Resignation

On this
cold October night
beside my windy fire
on Owasco's shore,

serenaded
by the hesitant whistle
of a single cricket,

the hollow slaps
of brown bass
breaking water,

the dull thud
of hickory
acorn and beech nuts
pounding the shore,

I realize
that although
this is the last night
this full moon
will be hidden
by oak leaves

I can still
look forward
to their branches
come winter

igniting
from one end
to the other
with so many
brighter more vibrant
leaves of stars

Speechless Among Stars

I am
breathing
stars

not their light
or
colder distance

but
the darkness
around their light

and its pull
from the bottom
of my words

at my sighs
below
gold stubble

spelling winter's
blackest
depths of snow

Life Signs

Almost winter
the cold
holds its breath

Icy Owasco
dims
its light of stars

In new snow
fallen
overnight

rabbit tracks
lead away
from the shore

With nothing
to console me
I follow them

Edge

At the edge
of the universe
is no edge

where not only
does
what exist for us
not exist

but apparently
there's no
end to this lack
of existence

even if
each of us
were to travel there
taking nothing
not even ourselves

even if
well before leaving
one of us
was to decide

who would be
the absence
and who would be

the emptiness
our hands would be
unable to let go of

Some Belief

Where
lightning cracks
its teeth
on Owasco's soft
waters

Where it
brightens the burrows
insects etch
under upturned bark

Where raindrops
adopt
the green of beech leaves
from which
goldfinches hang
and drink

Where the sum
of all differences
drifts between columns
it can never erase

I look up
as if I knew
where I was
as if I knew
the distance

from one star
to the next
could so easily
be erasing my name

Attraction

The slightest
sound of water
draws me near

walking
this stone road
downhill

and across
its foot bridge
above where

chattering
hummingbirds
blur
right past me

Readiness

The water's
sun
floats up
from its lake
bottom

Underwater
stones darken
its glowing
remains

the way features
of its ageless
face
like new flowers

look away
from the night
for the very
first time

Rescue

A shore fire
built
from driftwood

drawing wind
through a web
stretched across
the crushed
mouth
of a nearby
beverage can

after
trembling
through curly
yellow sandweed
blossoms

ignites
more hope
than any prayer
on my lips

could have ever
spilled
from a single drop
of light

A Night Vision

Full moon

and its stunning
reflection
across Owasco's
all but still water

resembling
a hive of light
around which
rapidly
weave and spin

brilliantly
winged swarms
of midnight's
golden brown
honeybees

Water Stone

Clear
to its bottom
of stones

Owasco
guides
full sunlight

along a path
below
its rocky
midday cliffs

kneading
and folding
this deep

light
on its water
into warm
loaves of waves

served
every few seconds
upon its shale
black shore's
unset table
to cool

Naming Silence

Before
it was nothing
hummed or
sung

was
sound
without
movement

silence
must have been

this still lake
across which
blue
dragonflies

and transparent
waterstriders
barely
ripple the vast
meaning

of their ever
widening
names

Lake Spider

A spider
strands its web

from the olive
green skin
of a fallen young
acorn

to the crimped
edge
of a cloud

in the blue sky
a rain filled
bottle cap

floats
and the wind
ripples

Silence, Silence

There is no
sound
over this silence

no
breathing
no
thoughtless voice

no
song simply
muffled
by falling leaves

no
single ripple
lapping
this shore
of broken shale

no
dry leaf veins
drifting
across this lake's
slow water

only
one stone
from under which
a string
of bubbles rises

and in black
circles
the reflection
of this new moon's
slender waist

Water Depth

On this
cold night
late
in October

an early snow
pirhouettes
powdery slippers
of wind
across Owasco's
rough surface

until its
see-through
body

spinning
and twisting
in a dance
among white lipped
waves

makes it
impossible to stop
speaking

about seagull
colored reflections
buried deep
in rusty boxes

among so many
summer moons
between the weedy
muck bottom
of its darkening self

Without Ever Going Back

Even though
I can't always see
the waves I hear
this early evening

Even though
I can't always feel
the energy
spring rains rush
down its feeder
stream's steps
of uneven stone
and slippery root

I'm still able to see
myself as that
fisherman's silhouette
guiding his skiff

among diamonds
the setting sun
harvests
from Owasco's
calm furrows of water

Apple Season in Central New York

This
is the morning's
stillness
in which my words

turn
taking the shape
of their objects

even
dance with me
armless
in a spin the twist

of an apple
off its leafy branch
taught me

when
hand-picked
and caught
in a wicker basket

the shape
of this
or any other
of my empty pages

Night Owl

A name
the owl calls
is not my name

but his own name
uttered
deep in the churn
of his throat

in the ruffle
of his feathered
neck
swiveling
from the call

his voice
in all directions
bounces back

off the earbones
brown
and gray-faced
field mice

fleeing
down starless holes
of earth
for a moment
point into the open
then vanish

Before Falling Asleep

What little
light of the moon
spruce pines
allow
through my window

taking the shape
of a colorless
butterfly's wingbeats

vanishes
then reappears
in the shape
of a much later hour

or a rain
wrapped sundrop
hanging
from the edge

of a yellow
strawflower's
stiff petal
cuddled
by a honeybee

Timed

Tonight
many of us lie
alone
in this darkness

between
ticks
of the clock

in whose gears
the teeth
of forgotten
hours

grind
our futures
to a halt

and where
in all
their hidden
wisdom

our dreams
barely keep us
from falling
back to sleep

Staying Put

I'm most fond
of this old
wooden chair's

splintered
frame creaking
beneath
my earth weight

whenever
I lean it back
against a south
facing wall

above which
bare
maple branches
overlap

and the voices
strong winds
rub
between them
speak up

as if to say
out here
night
perfects itself

An Unheard of Silence

Listening
to music end

all I think
I hear breathing
is myself

but silence
filling the room
is never alone

especially
when red spiders
hatching
from every
warm corner

emerge
stretching
their invisible
strands
connecting

one heartbeat
of mine
to the next

The One

I am
a circle
of one

who both
follows
and leads
myself

right after
bringing
myself back

from never
having
left

without
once getting
caught

by the speed
of my own
blood

Moth Sonatina

I like believing
this marbled
gray moth's dark
mosaic wings
are akin to mica
dug up
and rinsed off
in milky brown
mud puddles
as a child

Futility

Early evening's
pale sky
blossoms
between maple leaves
into stars

as if
there's more
than enough
night

each time
the still face
of this lake

stirred
then rippled
by weightless insects

upholds
how myths
are more times
than not

the tricks
our minds play on us
when first facing
the unknown

Memoire

A boy
remembers
how earth
lay flat
for as far
as he could see

and nights
were so dark
he believed he saw

more than one
rabbit flee
down the deepest
hole
in every star

Look No Further

Hands rub
gravel filled
mud
from a stone

until the glimmer
from a shine
off its wet skin

reveals
another light
living just inside
this stone

and which
to my surprise
turns out to be

my own eyes
which
when forced
to close

forgot
there was ever
the slightest
chance

they could ever
be one
and the same
as this stone
and open

Thirst

I cup
night
in my hands

sipping
from every
wrinkle and crack
between
its wobbly planets

a deep
blend of darkness
mixed
with just a sound
of water

where endless
reflections
of stars
are kept intact

and whose light
has never
been so quenching
as right now

Death Yet

The dead
stand at attention
next to my bed

Born
      naked
Buried
      naked

I watch as they
hold
cracked faces
up to the light

tinting
their broken
skin
a bloodless red

Born
      naked
Buried
      naked

From now on
dust
and its wind
will pray for me

From now on
instead of me
in my place

my absence
will finally be
at rest

Paul B. Roth lives in upstate New York with the sculptor Georgina Heksch Roth. A graduate of Goddard College in Plainfield, Vermont from which he also earned his Masters Degree in Contemporary French Poetry, he has been the editor and publisher of The Bitter Oleander Press since 1976, publishing contemporary poetry and fiction in translation, along with essays and interviews of substance about poetry and the creative act in both full length books and as a Spring and Autumn issued magazine.

In the late sixties, he studied poetry as an undergraduate at The University of Tampa with Duane Locke who is the undisputed founder of the Immanentist movement in North American poetry. There along with Steve Barfield, Alan Britt, Silvia Scheibli, and Nicomedes Suárez-Araúz, the movement coalesced and not surprisingly, still flourishes today in not only the United States, but in South American, Middle Eastern, Asian and European circles as well. Traditionally akin to the Surrealist and Deep Image movements of the past decades, Immanentism has given any poet who is willing, an engaging home in the ecstatic, visionary language of a highly nature based, particularized and associative poetry.

Roth's poetry is a mature blend of both sound and meditative images. There is a noticeably deep and measured breathing heard under the main tone in each of his poems. This breathing seems not so much that of the poet, but like that of the Earth. Perhaps the vibrations an earthworm might feel during a driving rainstorm might be something akin to this breathing. So, when he speaks, we have to listen carefully, for often it is a matter of his subtlety luring us deeper into his own imaginative blend of linguistic reality.

Other Books by Paul B. Roth:

After the Grape (University of Tampa Press-1969)
Basements of Tears (Ann Arbor Review Press-1973)
Half-Said (The Bitter Oleander Press—1976);
Nothing Out There (Vida Publishing, Inc—1996);
Fields Below Zero (Cypress Press—2002)
Cadenzas by Needlelight (Cypress Press—2009)
Words the Interrupted Speak (March Street Press—2011)
A Long Way Back to the End (Rain Mountain Press—2014)

www.ingramcontent.com/pod-product-compliance
Lightning Source LLC
LaVergne TN
LVHW040117080426
835507LV00041B/1394